My Sp... Book

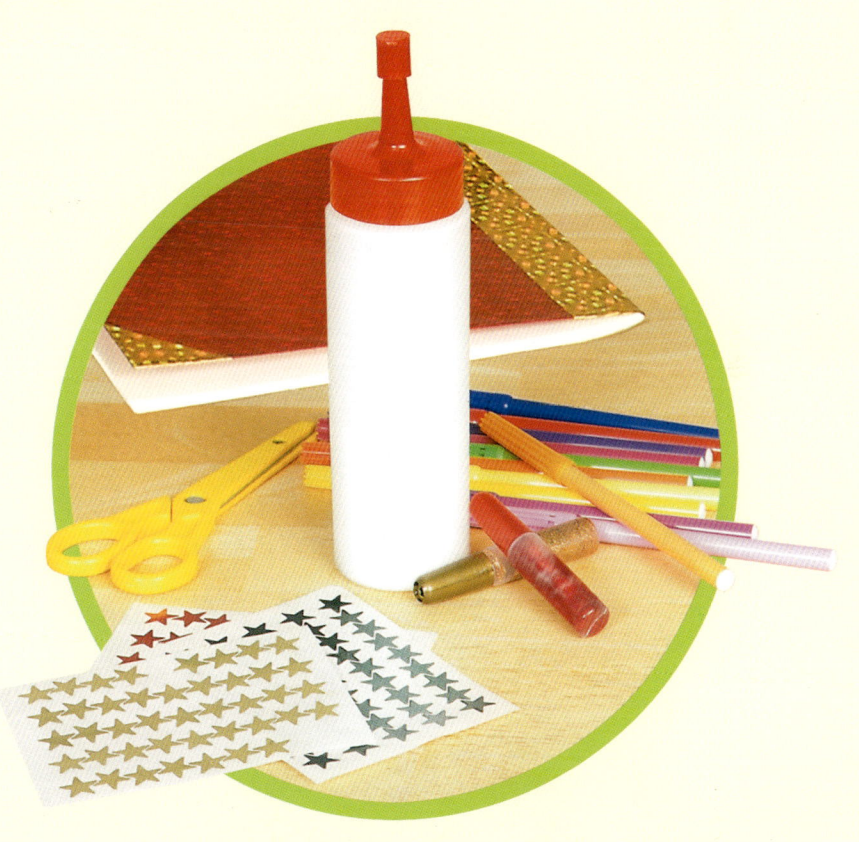

This is me
at the park.

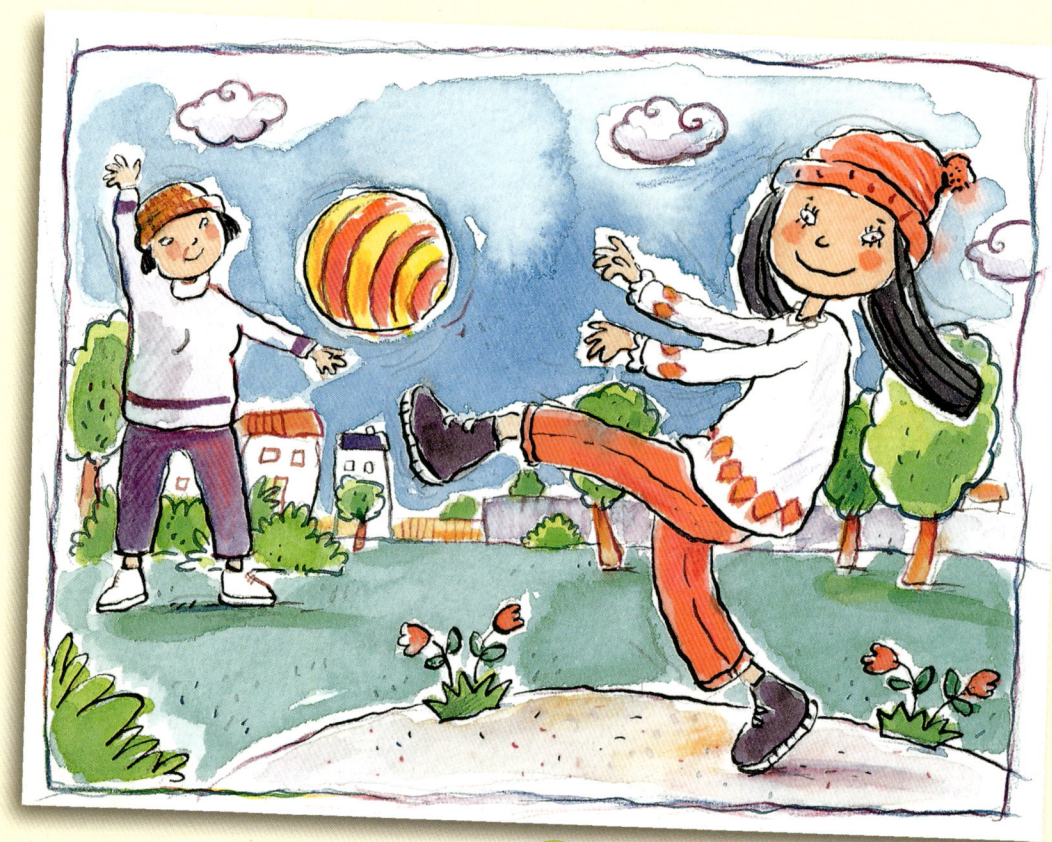

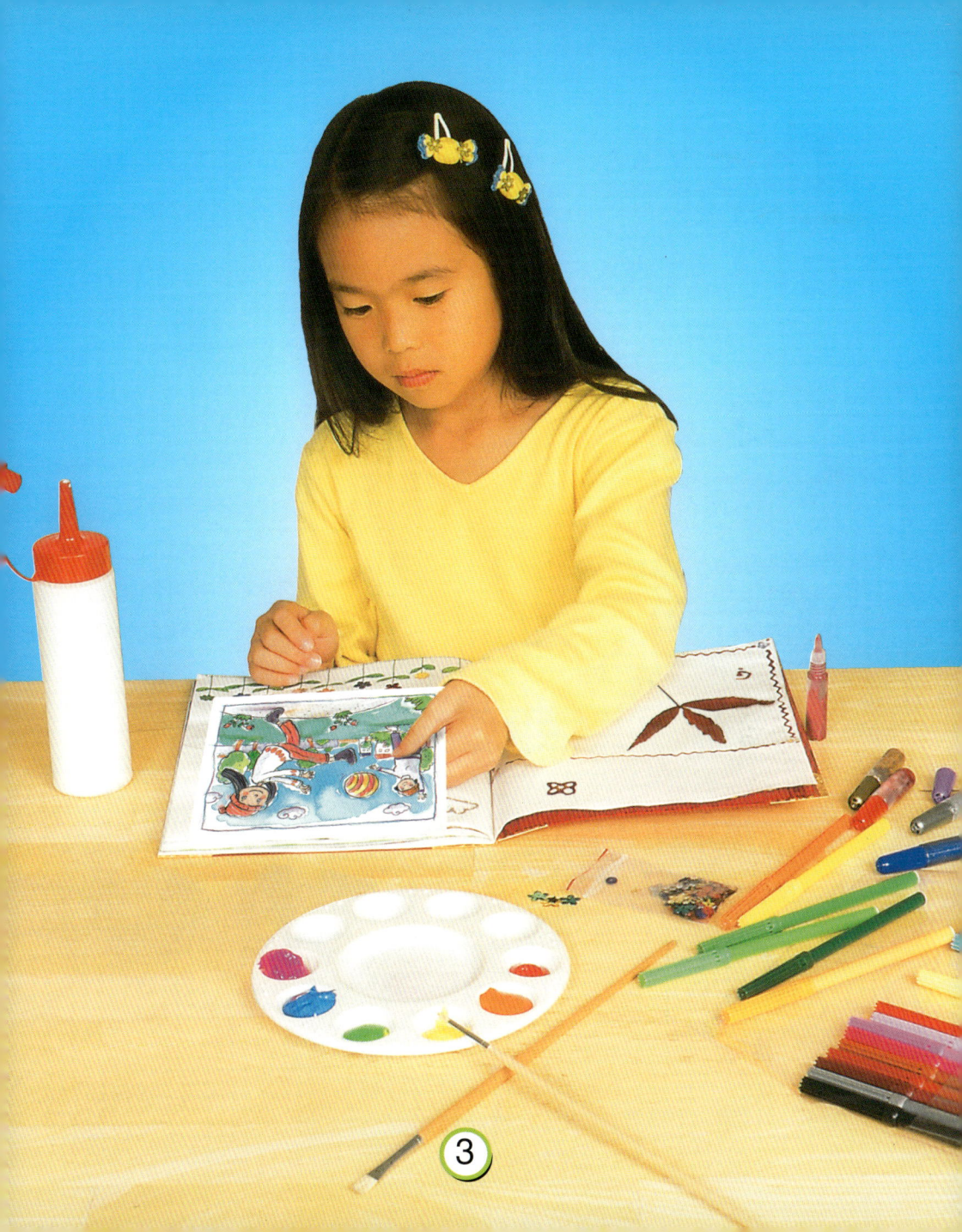

This is me at the shop.

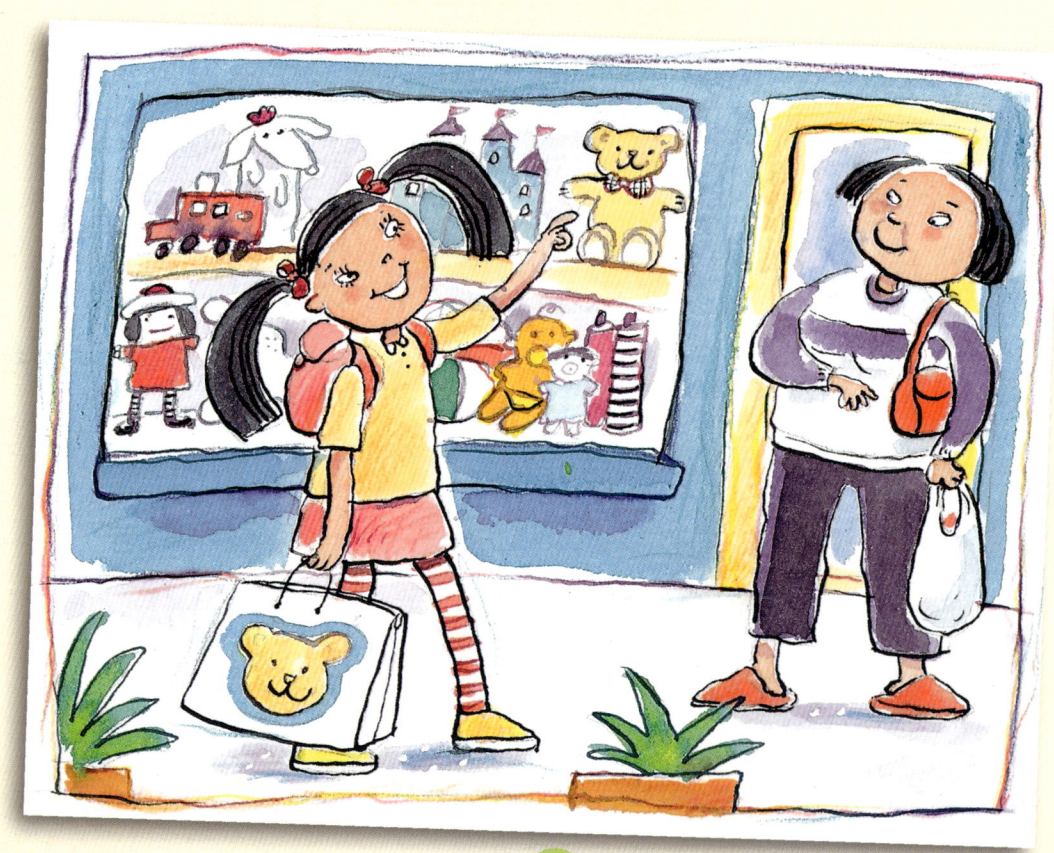

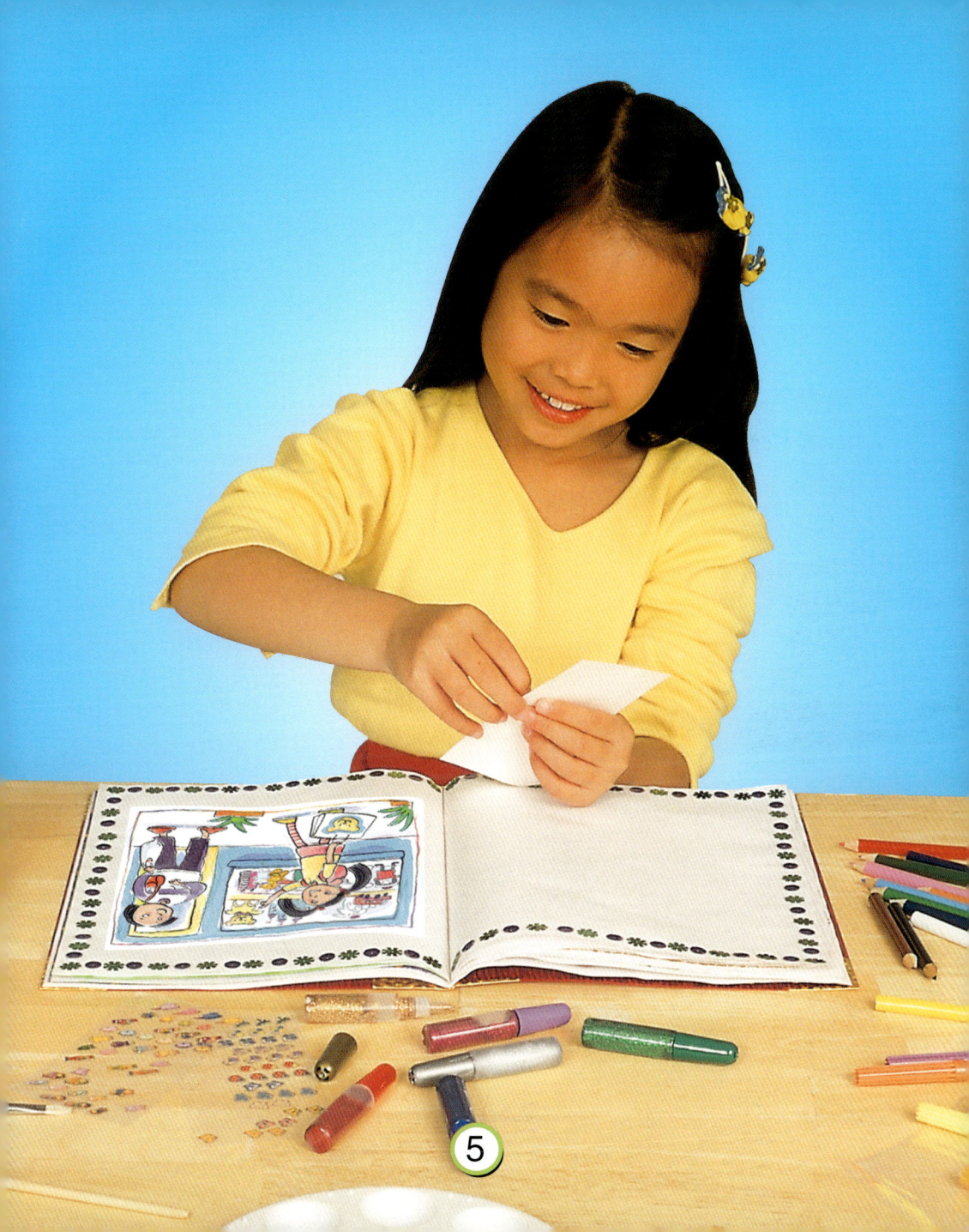

This is me at the pool.

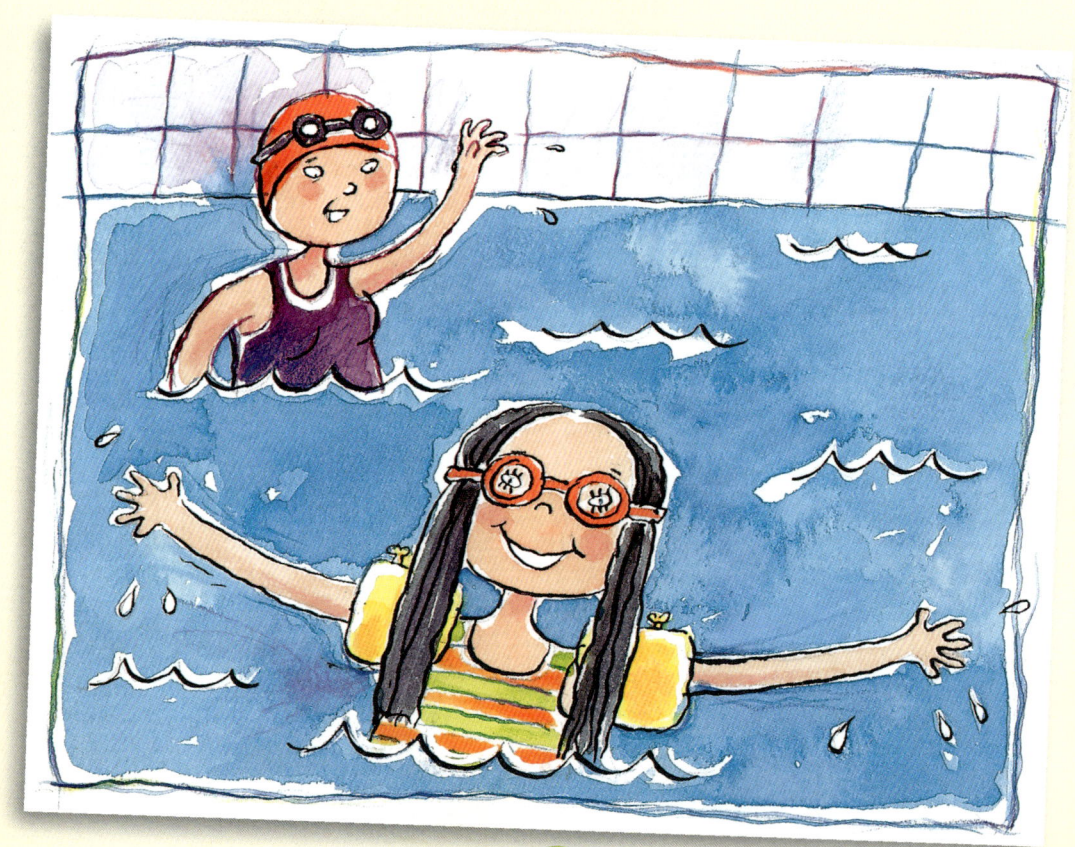

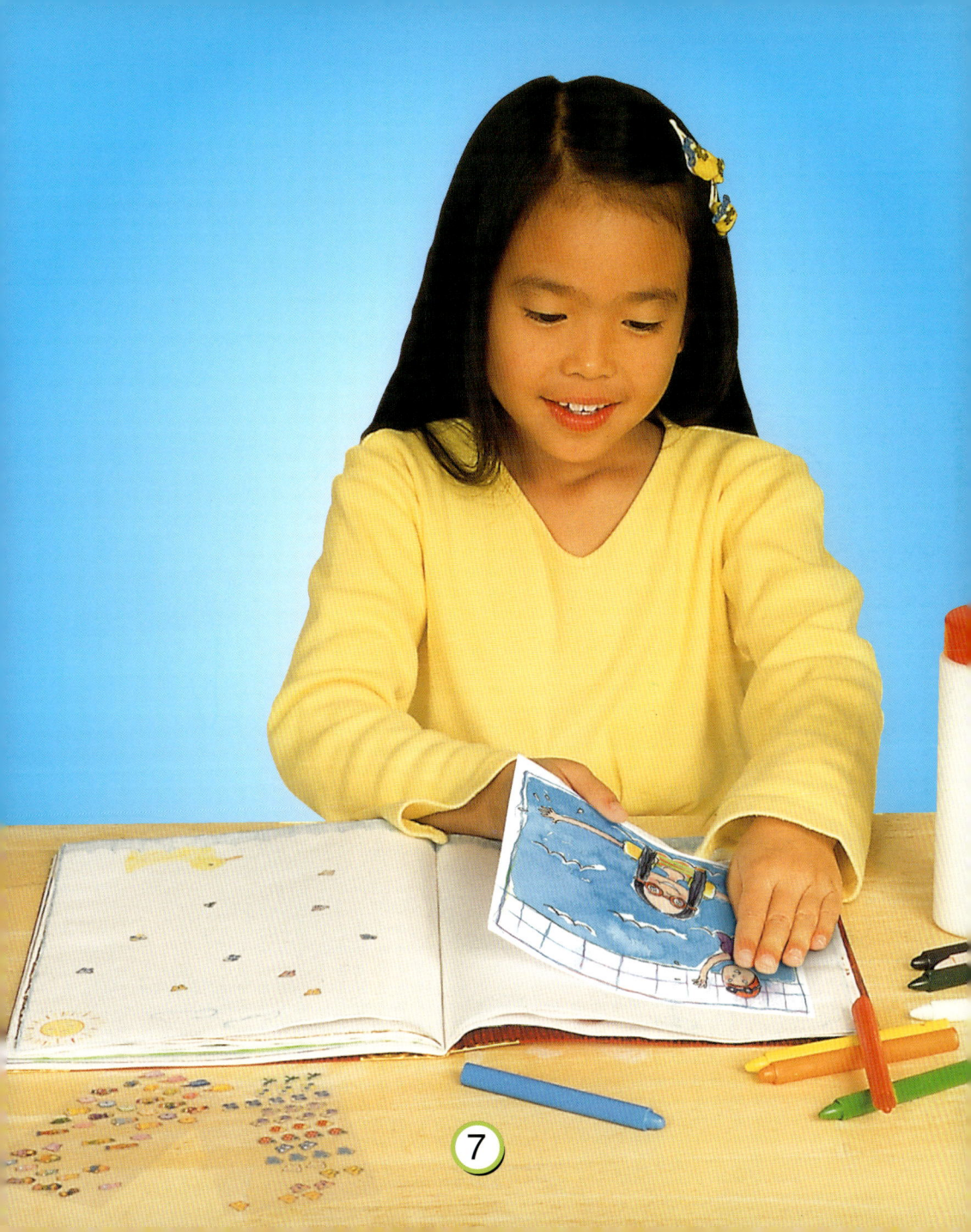

This is me
at the zoo.

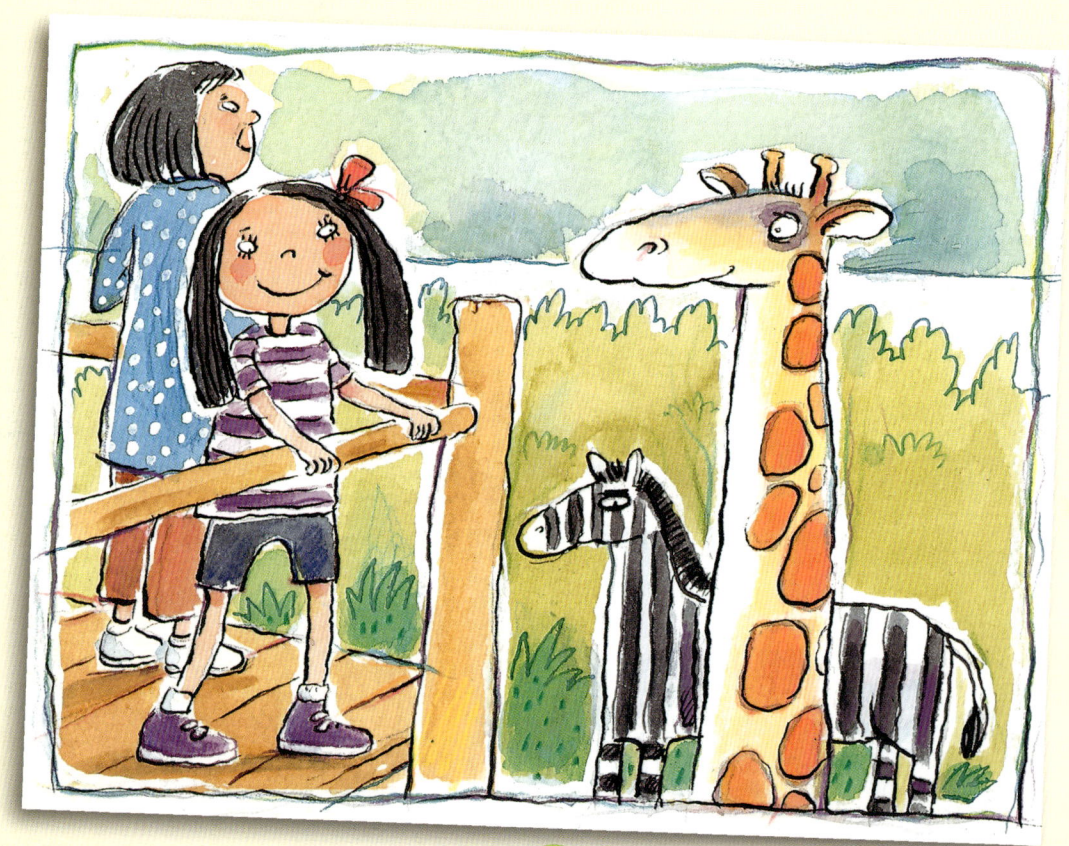

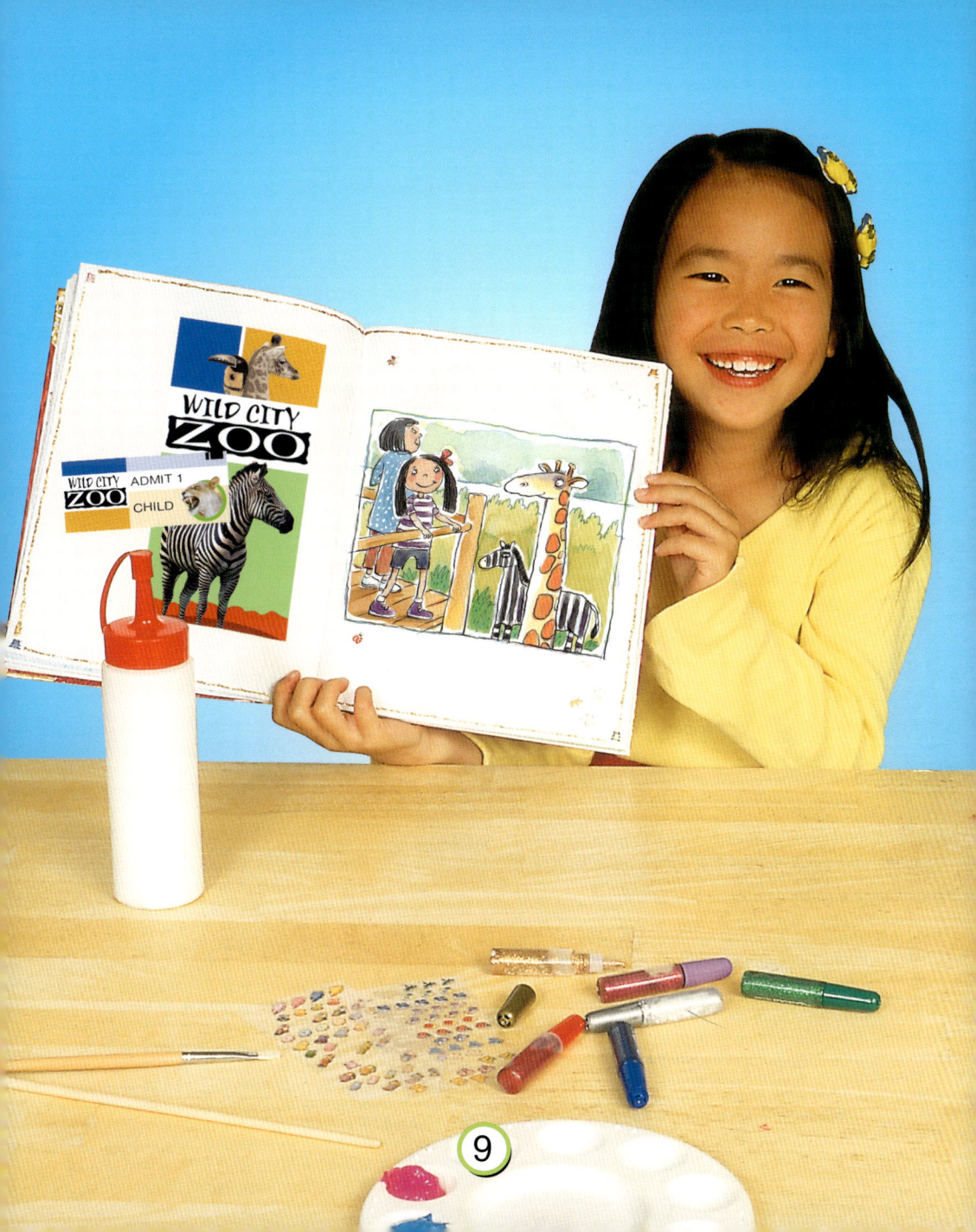

This is me at the library.

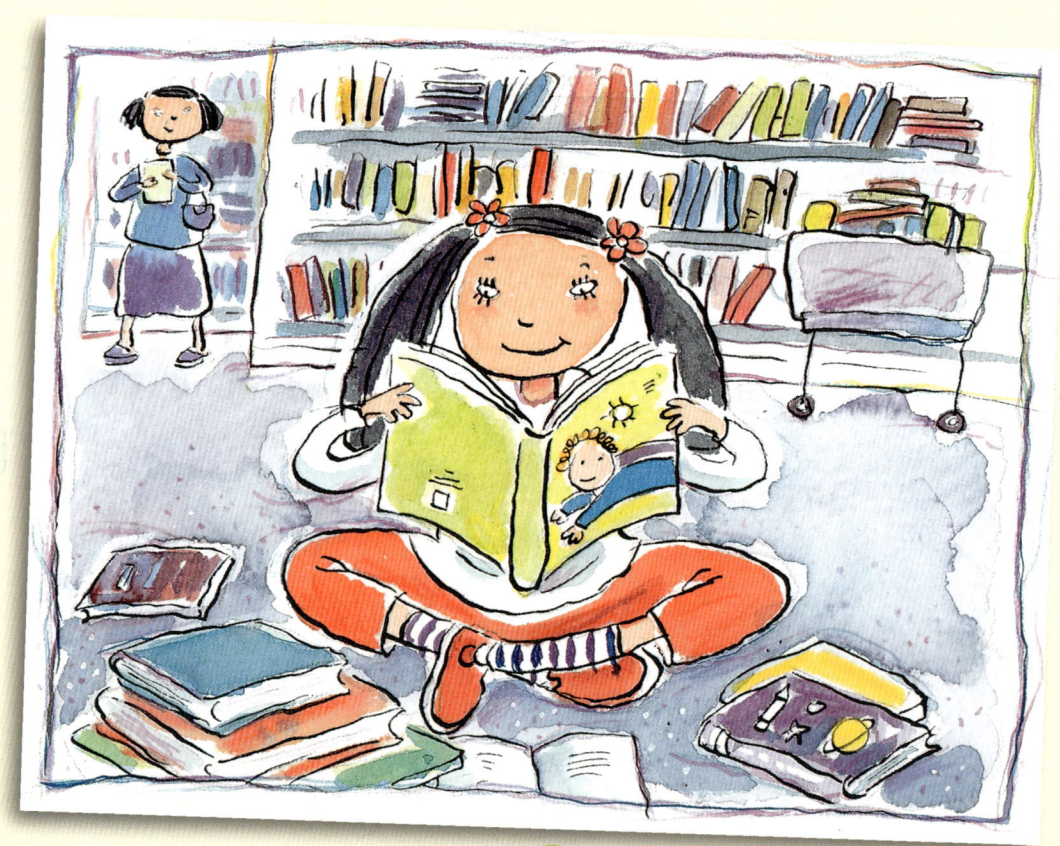

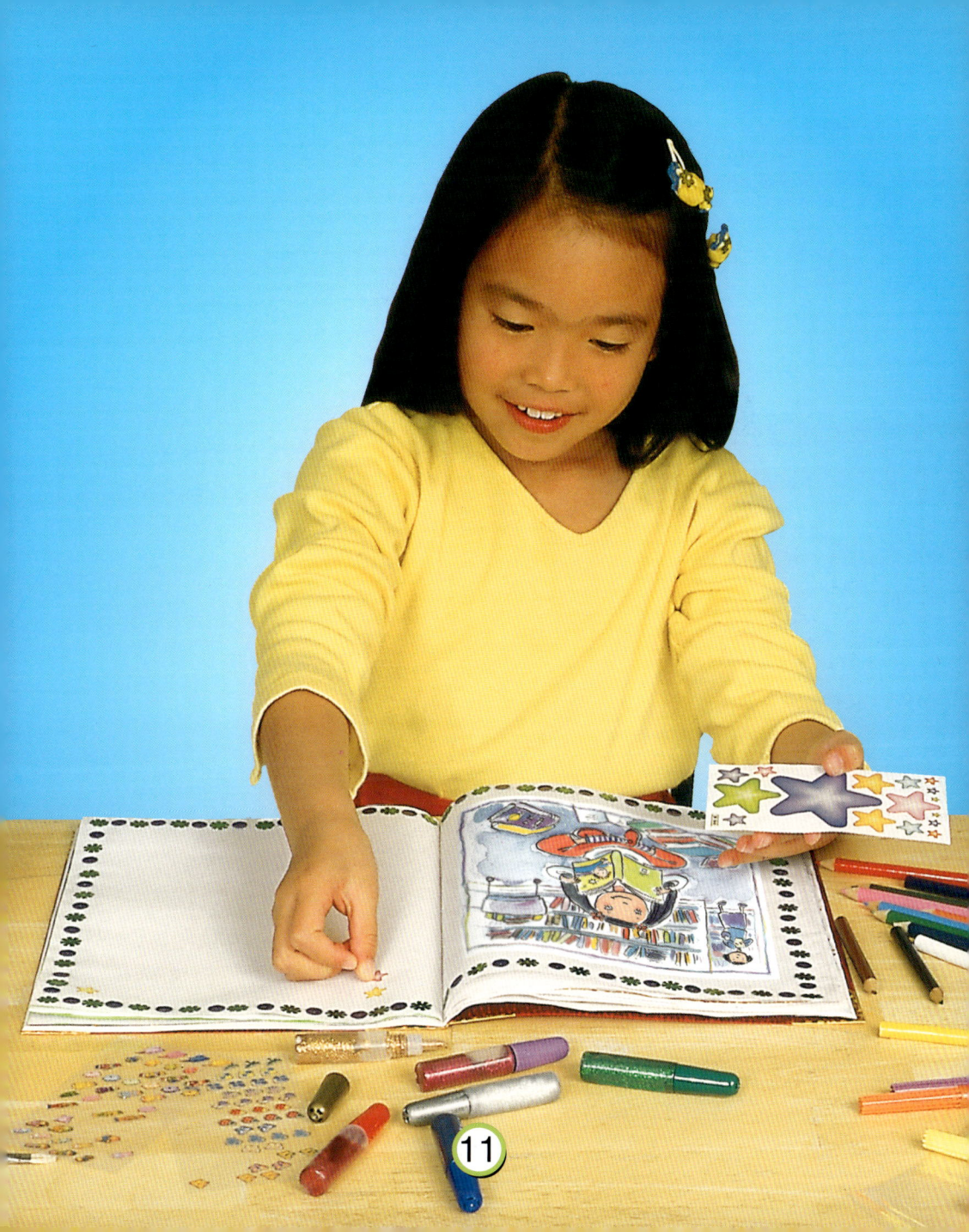

This is me at the playground.

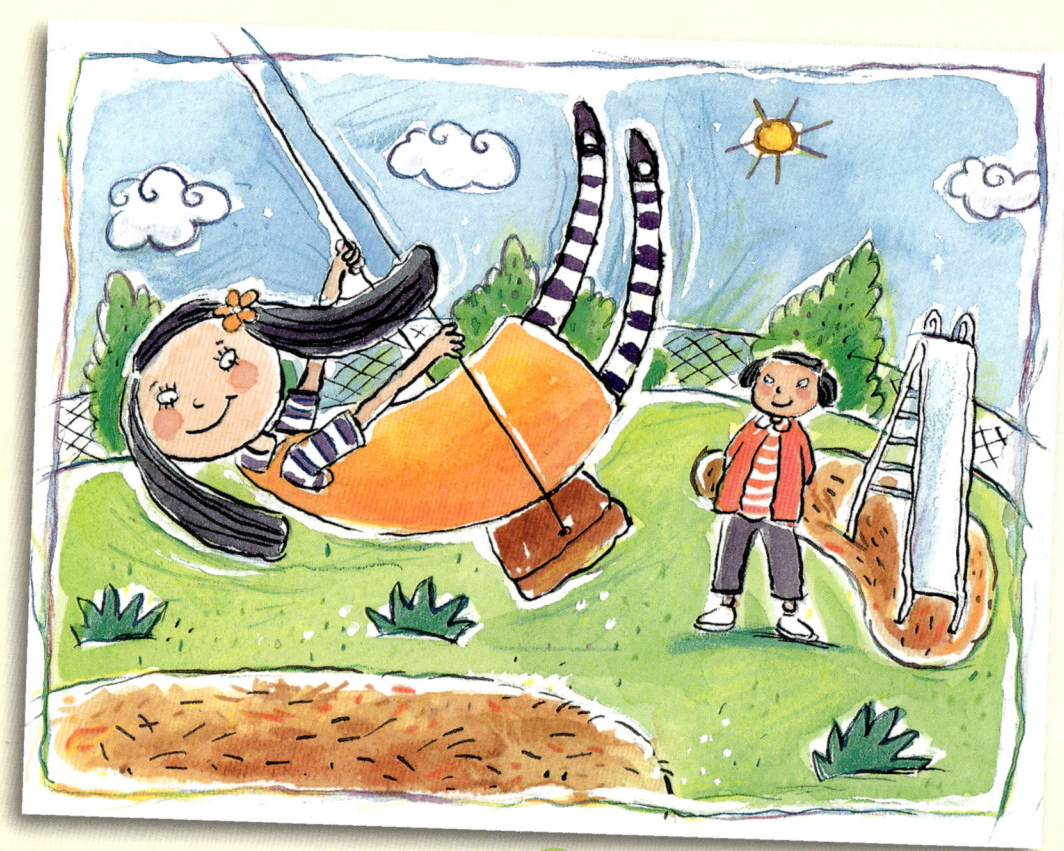

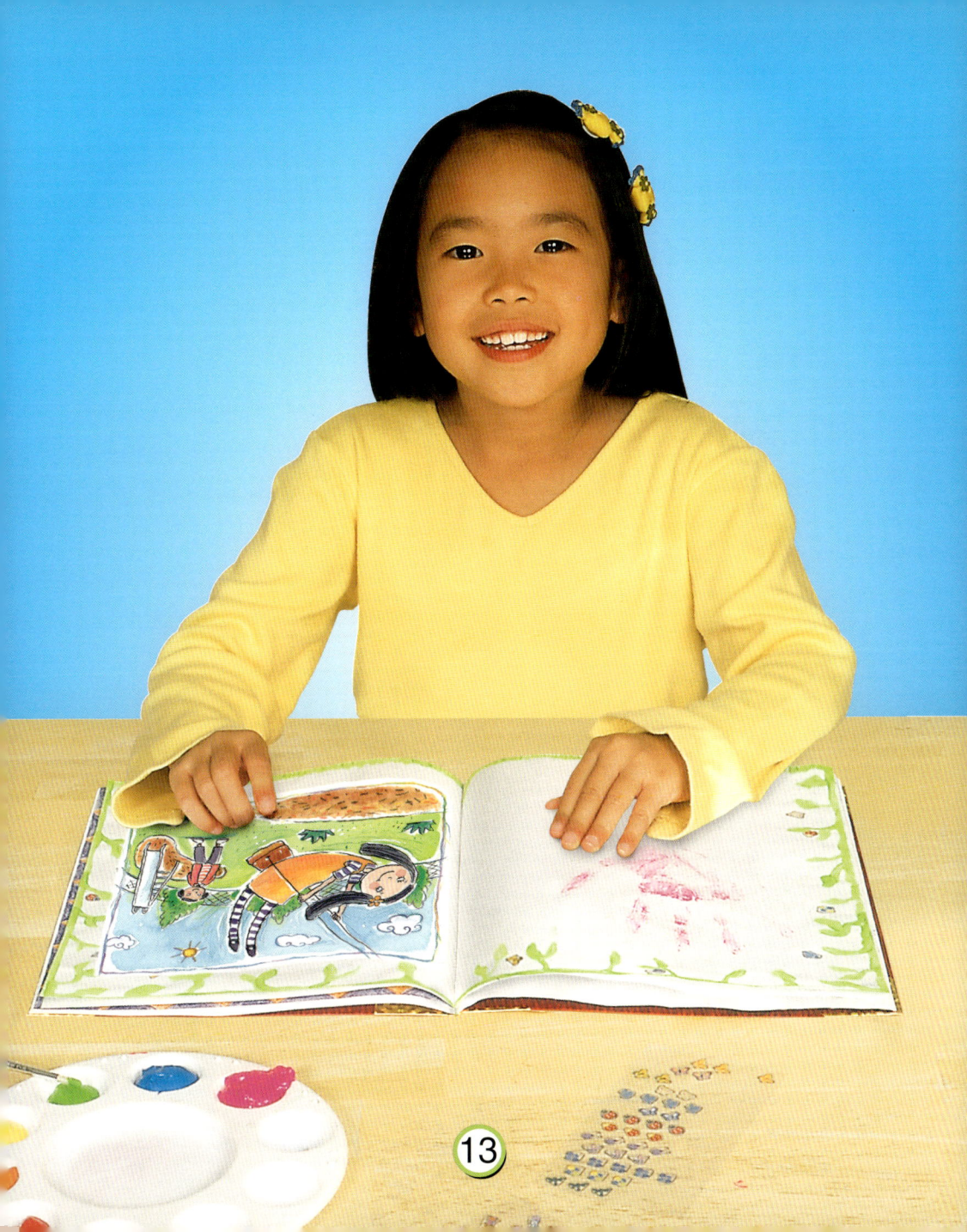

This is my map.

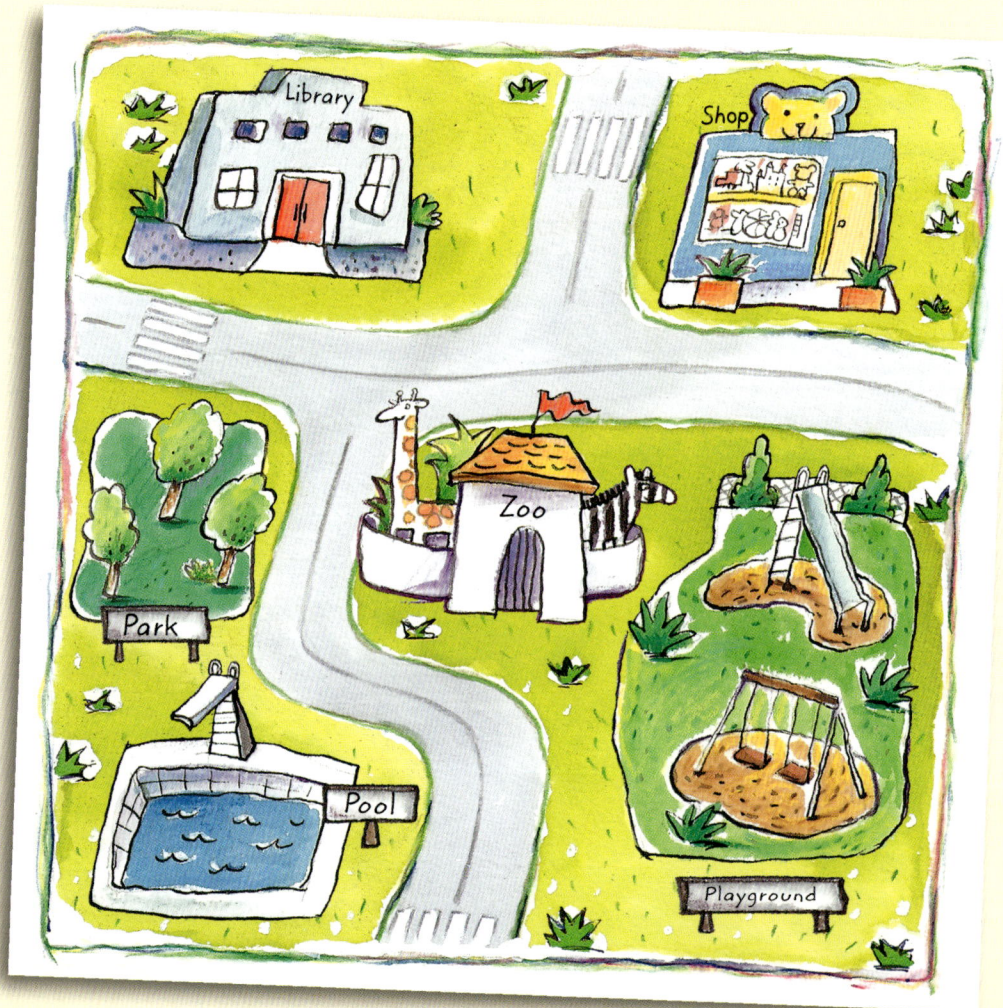

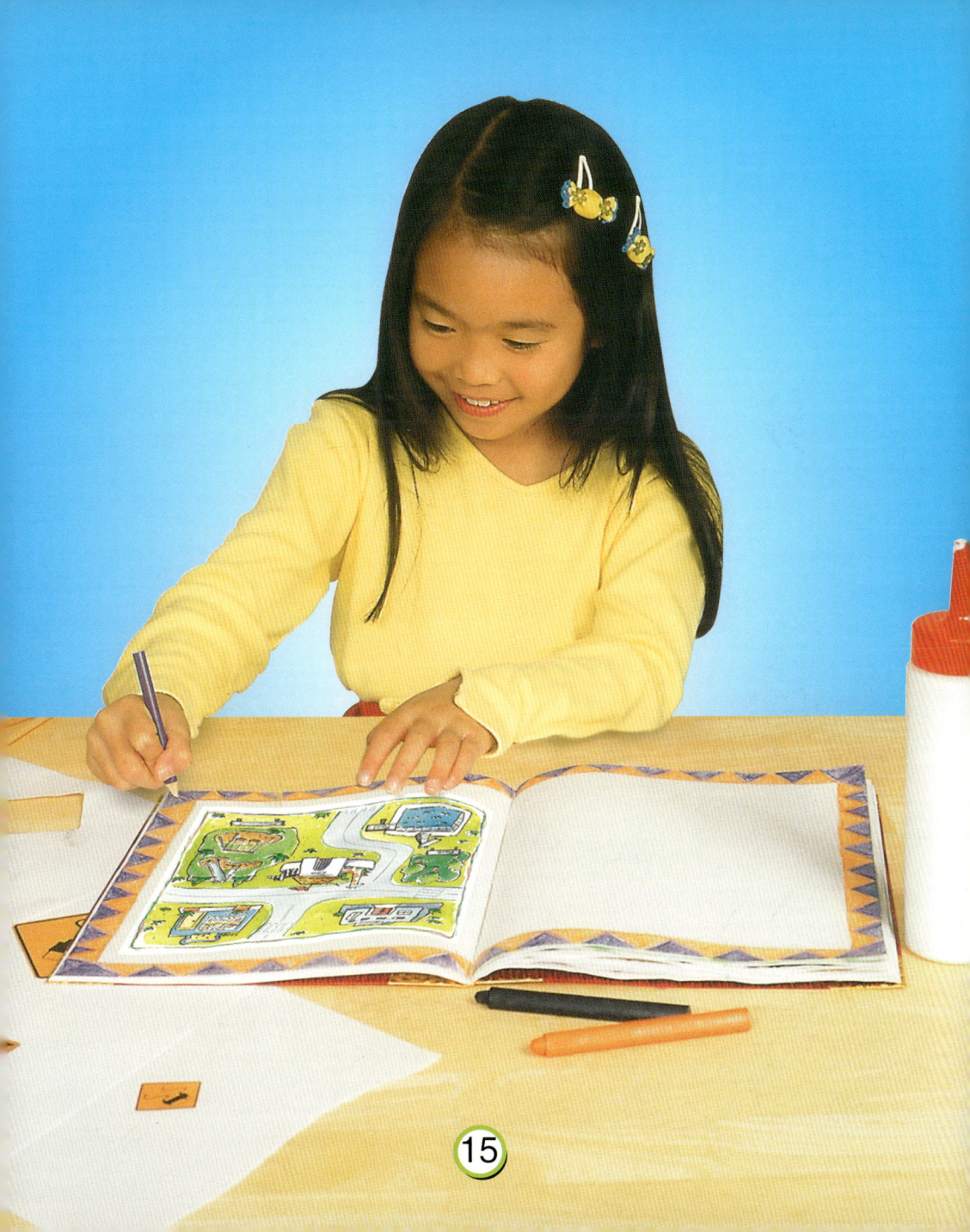

This is
my special book.

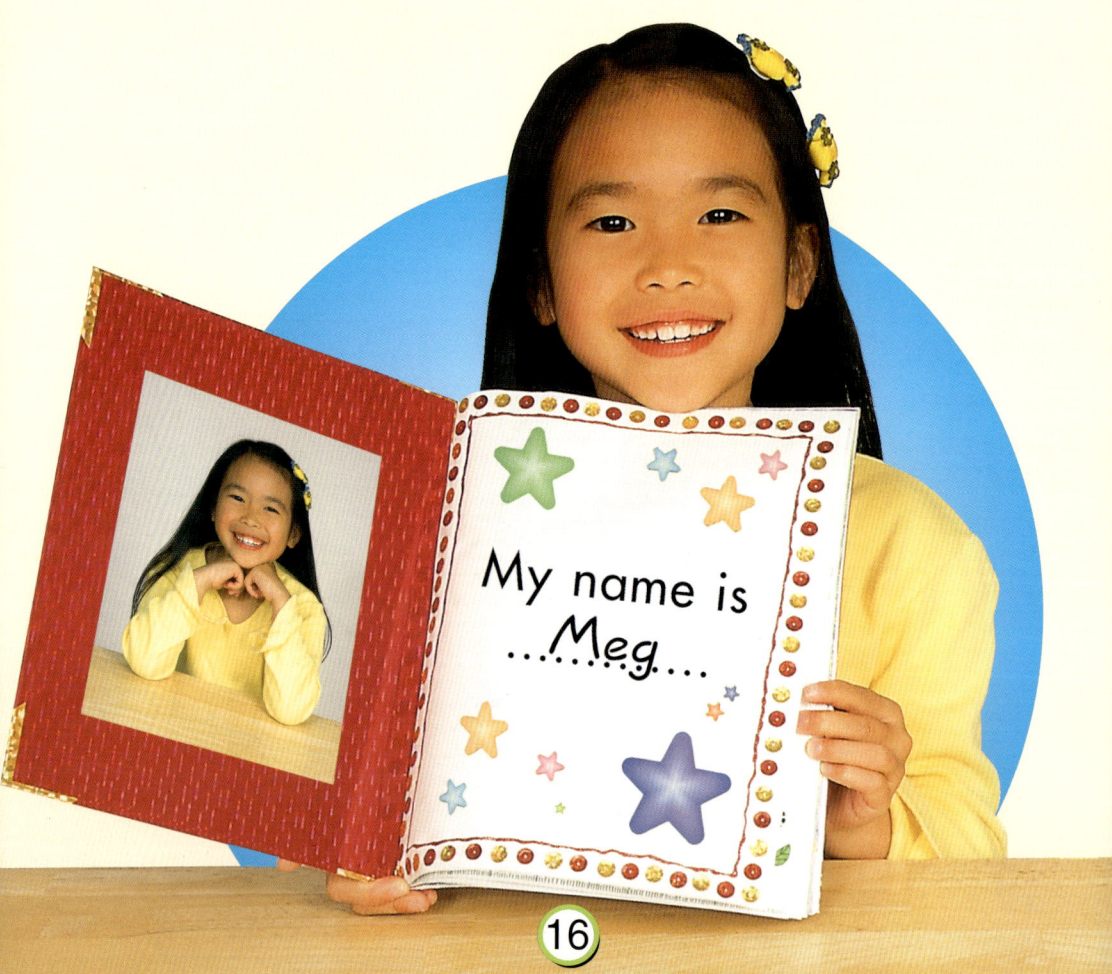